I Am

LEARNING TO WORK 'THE PRINCIPLES' FOR A BETTER LIFE

AN INTERACTIVE GUIDE

VMH Publishing
New York, NY

Manufactured in the United States of America

Paperback ISBN: 979-8-9869758-8-7
Hardback ISBN: 979-8-9869758-3-2
E-Book ISBN: 979-8-9869758-4-9

10 9 8 7 6 5 4 3 2 1

Publisher's Note:

The publisher is not responsible for the content of this book nor websites, or social media pages (or their content) that are not owned by the publisher.

LEARNING TO WORK 'THE PRINCIPLES'
FOR A BETTER LIFE

AN INTERACTIVE GUIDE

by
Dr. April Webster

Acknowledgments

I would like to thank my husband LaShawn Webster for his continued love and support. I could not have undertaken this journey without him. He believes in my ministry, and he pushes me beyond my limits. He is my strength when I am weak.

He brings me peace during any storm. He is the man that I prayed for, and God granted my request. He works the principles of faith with me daily and for that I am grateful. He is my everything and I am blessed to be his wife.

To my mother Shirley Wilson who is my best-friend, confidant, prayer partner and so much more. She introduced me to God at a young age. She taught me a lot of the principles you will read in this book. Because of her teaching, I have learned how to put these simple principles into action. I am grateful for our late-night talks and early morning prayers.

To my daughters Mahogany Grace and Nyjha, and my nieces Tristen and Mya, thank you all for being my inspiration and making me feel I can accomplish anything! I am aware that you all are watching me, and I plan to teach each of you everything that I know. You all will surpass my accomplishments and I'm looking forward to witnessing that day.

To my brothers Steve and Jarvis Wilson thank you for your unwavering support and unconditional love. You guys have always had my back and I'm thankful for both of you.

To everyone that will read this book. I pray you will work the principles provided and become aware of the I AM inside of you!

In this book, Dr. April Webster explores twelve affirmations to declare inward strength to her readers. *I AM* is a metaphysical name of the spiritual self. It is the presence of God with in you. When the words *I AM* are spoken it is a declaration. *I AM* is the mere fact of our existence and once you become aware of it you hold the power in your words. Dr. Webster has personally discovered the power of spoken words. This is not a book to be read only once then put away on a bookshelf or in a storage bin. This book is intended to be read and repeated over and over until one becomes fully aware of who they really are called to be. This book requires the readers to take action.

By following these principles, you hold the power of transforming your life to another level beyond your current position. Dr. Webster provides the steps needed to act and apply these principles to your life. You will walk and operate in another dimension once you become aware of who you really are. The words *I AM* represents your consciousness of who you are.

PRINCIPLE #1

I AM Destined To Win

There is greatness within you, and now is the time for it to come forth for others to see.

Before we get started, I would like to share my entrepreneur journey with you all. I have been an entrepreneur for over 10 years. The journey has not always been easy. I have had some crying days and sleepless nights. I want to take a moment to encourage someone whether you are in between jobs or career paths, or even trying to figure out what is your next step, I am going to share with you three principles that I believe you can utilize in this season. When you are destined to win, you must realize there will be some highs and lows. During this journey you will experience some ups and downs. You must realize God has equipped you with everything you need in order to win.

When I was getting started as an entrepreneur, I stepped out on faith and trusted God to lead the way. I didn't have anyone to teach me about being an entrepreneur. I had to figure it out on my own and through much fasting and praying. I started doing research. I started saving my money and I started investing in myself. Whatever you want to do in life it's going to require an investment. You are going to need to invest your time, invest your money, and invest your talents.

In 2006, I relocated to Memphis, Tennessee, without a job, just based on faith, and believing that God would open the door. I felt my education and resume would speak for me. But that did not happen. It took nearly six months for me to find a new career path. After a few years I felt I was being called to be an entrepreneur.

I am going to share with you the three principles that I have applied to my life, my business, and my ministry. After being in business for over ten years, I know these principles work. I still stand use them today and I believe they will help you, too.

The first principle I want you to share with you is, you must *remain Faithful*. Take a moment and write this principle in the note section provided. You must remain FAITHFUL! In the King James version of the Bible in Hebrews 11:1 it says, "Now Faith is the substance of things hoped for the evidence of things not seen." Please note it says Now Faith. Which means at this very moment. It's not referring to tomorrow or yesterday. But it means at his very present time and second. At this very moment that you are holding this book. You must have Faith to believe that there is greatness on the inside of you. It comes out by your faith.

Hebrews 11:6 says, "But without Faith, it is impossible to please HIM, for he who comes to God must believe that HE is, and that HE is a rewarder of those who diligently seek him. It's important for us to activate or FAITH NOW. By Faith we see the world called into existence by God's word, what we see created by what we don't see.

Albert Einstein has a quote that says, "Imagination is everything. It is the preview of life coming attraction." It first starts in our mind. Whatever you want to do in life, whatever you want to become, it first starts with a thought in your mind."

It first starts in our minds. I remember having a meeting with the CEO of a company similar to the one I own today. As I was sitting there I had a thought that one day I'm going to own a company like this one. The idea first started in my mind. It was literally six years later I opened a business similar to the one I had worked at for several years. I stayed faithful to my dream and goals. I didn't get discouraged when it didn't happen overnight. But instead I continued to work harder.

I want to encourage you not to give up when things do not go the way you have planned. That means you cannot give up on your dreams and vision. When things get tough, you cannot quit. You must continue working the principles by applying them to your daily life.

The second principle that I want to share is you must *remain Fearless*. Take a moment and write this principle in the note section. Now, being fearless is understanding who you are called to be and understanding your why. When you are fearless you will not allow people or situation to put you in a box.

When you are fearless, you realize even through trial and tribulation, or whatever it is that might come your way, you are going to prevail. I realized I was fearless when I started entering rooms and spaces and allowing my presence to be known. A fearless person doesn't allow the opinions of others to hinder them from reaching their goals. When you are fearless, you will not allow anything to hold you back. My husband, LaShawn says it like this, "You must stand on your square."

Faith and Fear cannot operate together. You will have to choose one over the others. So, I encourage you to apply both by being Faithful and Fearless. For the past 20 years every morning I start my day with Morning Devotion. I understand the words written in 2 Timothy 1:7 King James Version that says, "God has not given us the Spirit of fear but of power, love, and a sound mind."

The third principle is *remain Focus*. You must be focused on reaching your goals. You have to be willing to give it all you got in order to accomplish your dreams and visions. To be focus requires you to concentrate on it and think about it daily. It should be at the top of your thoughts. You can not allow any distractions to get in our way to take you off course of reaching our goals. Focus requires your undivided attention. To be focus you must invest time into whatever you are trying to accomplish and achieve. I want to end this chapter with a poem on staying focus by Bill Kochman.

"Stay focused, you've got a job to do, stay focused, ignore the Devil's boo. Stay focused, through the lions roar, stay focused, lead folks to the Door. Stay focused, when the naysayers bite, stay focused, you will win this fight.

Stay focused, your eyes upon the Lord, stay focused, hold tightly your sword. Stay focused, through waves crash down. Stay focused, you will get your Crown. Stay focused, the battle's almost won, stay focused, behold the light of dawn."

Grab Your Pen & Work The Principle

I AM Destined to Win

May God bless you. May God keep you. That is my prayer, in the name of Jesus.

PRINCIPLE #2

I AM A Warrior

As a warrior, we are committed to having a "can-do" attitude. You understand that you can do whatever you set your mind to. There is nothing that will stand in your way. This chapter is geared to speak to the warrior within you. Whatever you are facing today, now is the time to dust your shoulders off, stand up, and arise to the occasion.

I love the way Merriam-Webster dictionary describes the word arise. It means, to rise up or get up. On today, arise knowing this is a new day, one that wasn't promised to us. Every day, we are given another opportunity to impact the world. I am calling for you to arise and put on the whole armor of God. As a warrior, we are sometimes faced with battles or situations.

There will be times when we go through situations, trials, or tribulations. As warriors we must maintain our posture. Do you realize we have the tools we need to survive. When we were born God gave us everything, we would need in this lifetime.

As a Warrior, we must always be prepared to act. We prepare for war, for the storm, for battles. When the forces of our will are aligned with the creative spirit within us, a warrior stands the test of time.

When I use the word warrior, that is not limited to only those who physically go fight in a battle or war, it can also be those who are prayer warriors who are standing in the gap and interceding for their family and friends. It could be somebody who is a mediator, who is going to make the intercessions for things to come. It could be the person in the business who you are going to be encountering that have been assigned by GOD to get you to your next level by Faith.

Understand we have Warriors who are assigned to assist and help us. I can recall a time when I came in contact with a person that informed me they had been praying and interceding for me. She started sharing different situations that had occurred in my life and how she had been praying for me.

I did not know her personally and we do not talk often. But she felt God had given her instructions to pray and intercede on my behalf. On today, I want you to know if you're reading this book, I have been praying for you. I have prayed over this book and everyone that will hold it in their hands. My prayer is that the principles in this book will ignite a fire in you to arise to the occasion. There are gifts and talents that have been lying dormant, and now is time for you to Arise.

Today is a new day to start fresh. Allow this chapter to speak to the warrior inside of you. Do not allow another year to pass and your gifts and talents have not come fourth. Now is the time and the hour for you to put the pen to the paper. Start writing your visions and making it plan. Apply the principles from this book and allow the journey to begin. Arise Warrior destiny is calling.

Grab Your Pen & Work The Principle

I AM A Warrior

____
____
____
____
____
____
____
____
____
____
____
____
____
____
____
____
____
____
____
____
____
____
____
____
____

May God bless you. May God keep you. That is my prayer, in Jesus name.

PRINCIPLE #3

I AM Fully Persuaded

In Romans 8: 38-39, from the King James Version, says, "I am persuaded that neither death nor life nor angels nor principalities, nor powers, nor things present nor things to come, nor height, nor depth, nor any other creature, shall be able to separate us from the love of God, which is in Christ Jesus our Lord."

I would like you to write these words: *I am fully persuaded.* In this life all of us will experience some type of hardship. Trust me, no one is exempt from encountering ups and downs. But please note, no matter what problem, circumstance, or situation comes our way nothing will ever separate us from the love of Christ.

I remember when I lost my father in 2022. I was in my hometown of Hickman, KY for the weekend and I went into the convenience store. While I was looking for a particular item a woman came up to me. She said, "Oh it is you." I heard about your dad. She proceeded to give me condolences and then she asked, are you still preaching? I paused for a moment before I answered. Then I answered by saying, absolutely. My dad knew that I was called to be an Evangelist. He was actually very proud of me. He would tell everyone, my daughter is a preacher and she is good. He would not want me to stop preaching the good news because life happened. Nothing should ever keep us from doing what we are called to do.

I am fully persuaded God called me to be an Evangelist, Entrepreneur, and an Empowerment leader for women. Are you fully persuaded in your calling or who you are destined to be? If not, that is completely fine. You still have time to discover your purpose. In the note section that is provided in this chapter write down 3 things that you are fully persuaded God has called you to do in this lifetime.   I already provided my three at the beginning of this paragraph. As you write those three items also include a reason for each of them.

In Romans the 8th chapter Paul provides us with a list. I will only go over a few of the items in this chapter. The first one, he said that I am fully persuaded that 'neither death nor life shall separate us from the love of God." I just mentioned that my father Calvin transitioned in 2022. Death will separate the soul from the body. But death cannot separate us from the love of God. In fact, death is not a separation, but a return to the father. When my father passed away, I couldn't understand it. Things happened so quickly. We almost didn't have time to process everything. I remained faithful, fearless, and focused. I didn't allow the separation to hinder me from doing the will of the Lord.

Paul even says, "I am fully persuaded, nor things present, nor things to come". No matter what happens, no matter what comes to pass, what you believe, or you do not believe, if you agree or disagree, nothing will ever separate us from the Love of God.

We are in the middle of an uneasy time right now. If you are reading this book, then you understand that we survived the Covid 19 Pandemic that started in March 2020. Hard times happen in this world. It's not the first time and it will not be the last time. It's important to have complete faith in God. Just as God was with the children of Israel in the desert, during the 40 years and various seasons, he will be with us.

There isn't anything that we have done, could have done, should have done. Life happens to all of us and things will come and go. We will see good and bad while on this earth. But there is good news on today! Nothing can separate us from the LOVE of God.

I want to end this chapter in prayer. Please take time and read this prayer out loud.

Dear Lord, thank you for your unconditional love. We are fully persuaded that nothing will ever separate us from your love and your protection. *This is going to be our season of greatness. We will walk into all you have given us with complete conviction, that we have gifts and talents that needs to come forth in this season. God thank you for the tools you have given us. Thank you for more knowledge and wisdom. Thank you for giving us the ability to create wealth. Thank you for new ideas and witty inventions. In all that we do we will give you the Glory and the honor.*

I pray this in this season we are completely aware of your presence, knowing you are with us every step of the way. Even if we walk through the valley of the shadow of death, and things seem like they are not going to happen in their lives, God, you are with us. Continue giving us assurance that everything is working for our good.

God, I thank you that there will be no shortage, there will be no setbacks. There will be no more second-guessing ourselves. There will be no more wondering about it. But we are completely convinced this is the moment, and the time is now. God, we are totally convinced you are going to be there with us every step of the way.

So, God, *I thank You for this day. I thank you to each and every reader who is using I AM and Working the Principles. I thank you for every person that purchased a copy of this book. God bless their hands even the more. Allow everything that they touch in this season brings them a return on their seeds.*

I pray that your days will continue to be blessed, and you will thrive in all things that your hands touch. May God bless you, and may God keep you. That is my prayer in Jesus name.

Grab Your Pen & Work The Principle

I AM Fully Persuaded

May God bless you. May God keep you. That is my prayer, in Jesus name.

PRINCIPLE #4

I AM Shifting

I AM Shifting. As I was preparing this message, immediately I thought about a vehicle. All vehicles no matter the make, model, size, or color all offer at least three to four gears shifters. Which are called park, reverse, drive, and neutral. I'm going to use those as categories on today.

We all know if you place your vehicle in park, you are not able to move. You are literally placed in one position. Now, if you decide to shift gears, you have several options. You can choose to shift to drive which will allow you to move forward or you can shift into reverse which will allow you to move backwards. These two options allow you to start moving. Then you have the last option to shift into neutral. In neutral you are no longer moving again but you have the ability to move if someone assist or pushes you.

I want to urge everybody that is reading these words, it is time to shift gears and start moving forward.

I want to bring your attention to a passage in the King James version of the Bible. In Luke 5th chapter verse 4-7 reads below.

4. Now when he had left speaking (Jesus), he said unto Simon (Peter), Launch out into the deep, and let down your nets for a draught.

5. And Simon (Peter) answering said unto him, Master, we have toiled all the night, and have taken nothing: nevertheless, at thy word I will let down the net.

6. And when they had this done, they enclosed a great multitude of fishes: and their net brake.

7. And they beckoned unto their partners, which were in the other ship, that they should come and help them. And they came, and filled both the ships, so that they began to sink.

Simon (Peter) was put into as situation. He is a fisherman by trade. He knows the ropes of fishing. That is what he has always done, and yet, he finds himself in a situation that his skills and tools are no longer working in his favor. Here we have a skilled fisherman that isn't able to catch any fish. The scripture tells us that he has been working all night and have caught nothing.

Some of you may be able to relate to this situation. You have been working at a certain career and it seems as if you are not progressing. You are at the point where you feel you have tried everything and nothing is getting better or moving forward. Whatever your case might be, it's time to shift gears. May I encourage you on this day, as Jesus told Peter in the boat launch out into the deep and cast your net to the other side.

Simon (Peter) is considered a skilled fisherman by trade. He knows how to do it, when to do it, and what to do. He understands the principles of fishing. But he finds himself in a situation where none of his skills and knowledge are working. But, he is given a word by Jesus to launch out into the deep and cast his net to the other side. He obeyed the word of the Lord and was able to catch so much fish that he needed assistance from others.

I want you to think about that passage. Have you found yourself in a similar situation like Simon (Peter). If so, is it time for you to shift your thinking and say, nevertheless at thy word. The same principles that Jesus taught Simon and the disciples that were watching still apply to us today. There may come a time in your life that you will simply have to launch out into the deep. In the deep water you must trust and depend on the Lord.

I would like to challenge you to expand your mindset in this year. Understand that it is going to require you to shift gears. Stop being in park wondering what if? How do I do this? No, no, no. That's over. Start writing out the vision; start moving forward with the plan that you have.

When Peter cast his net over to the other side, you know what? Not only did he catch fish, but he also caught multiple the amount, so much that he had to call for the other fisherman to come and help him. That's the type of blessings waiting for us when we launch out into the deep.

Remember this, as you prepare to launch out into deep waters, you must have confidence in knowing God is with you. Launching out into the deep requires having Faith. Hebrews 11:1 says, *'Now, faith is the substance of things hoped for, the evidence of things not seen.'* Hope is a testimony to things unseen.; walking by faith rather than by sight. We must shift in our thinking. Shift in our talking and Shift in our Speaking.

When Peter went forth to go into deep waters, he did not ask questions of God. He said, Yet, nevertheless, he went with a net and he cast it to the other side. I want to encourage you on this day, it is time for a change your way of thinking right now. It is your time now to shift. Do not hesitate. Do not ponder on it. The change must happen. We are moving forwards, and not going backwards anymore. We are not going in reverse. No turning back, no U-turns, absolutely nothing. We are shifting gears, shifting mindsets, shifting faith. I want to challenge you to write this words on the note section of the chapter, *I AM SHIFTING.* While you are writing also say it out loud.

When you start shifting you make room for more. More blessings will come to you when you have the capacity to receive it. Know that God loves you. It is time to put our faith into action. Faith without works is dead, so simply know that the time has come for you to shift gears and move forward.

I pray you will speak these words into your life. I am touching and agreeing with you. *I AM SHIFTING!!!*

Grab Your Pen & Work The Principle

I AM Shifting

May God bless you. May God keep you. That is my prayer, in Jesus name

PRINCIPLE #5

I AM Staying in My Lane

It is very important to stay in your own lane in this season. Let me give you an example of why this principle is important. Around the year of 1996, I use to run track. We had a real good track team, and we won our district which caused us to advance to the Regional Tournament. We were so excited for the opportunity, and we had a very humble team. During my track years I ran the 4x100 relay and the open 200. Our relay team was scheduled early in the morning. We were ready and prepared to run our race.

I can remember hearing the gun sound and my teammate took off. I ran the third leg so I could tell we were in second place. When she handed me the baton, I remembered being nervous, but I was determined to run with all my power, all my stamina, all I had in me. I handed the baton to my friend, and I noticed she was getting tired, but she continued running, she keeps going, and, oh, my God, we came in second place which would allow us to advice to another bracket. But then our Coach came over to us with a strange look on his face. Suddenly, he started looking at us and said, 'Girls, you did great.' You know, full of energy and happiness. 'But we knew there was something wrong.' He started saying one of the judges reviewed everything and one of us had stepped out of our lane.

We had crossed over into someone else lane. Now, do I believe that we should have been disqualified? No. But guess what happens in life. All of us are given a race to run, and you need to remember to stay within your own lane. Do not let distractions cause you to look to the left or right. Concentrate and focus on the race you are scheduled to run.

In the King James Bible in the book of Ecclesiastes 9:11, it says, *the race is not given to the swift or to the strong, but to the one who*

39

endures until the end. Let me encourage you on this day, no matter what race you are running, you must run it with all of you might.

You must remember that your race is for you to run. I want to provide 3 tips in this chapter. The first tip that I want to provide is, *Stay centered on your goals.* Our goal was to win the race and come home as champions. But our story did not end that way and that will happen in life. It is important that no matter what obstacles come in your path you stay centered on your goal. Let me tell you how to center your mind. Centering your mind means requires us to bring calmness to our emotions. During our race our emotions were all over the place. We were anxious, nervous etc. But it's important to keep your mind in a calm state of being. You must be Present, you must be Aware, and you must be determined that whatever comes your way, you will run your race with style and grace, and run your race until the end.

Today, I am passing you the torch. When you receive the baton, whether it is a baton to start your business, whether it is a baton to lead others, whether it is a baton to return to school, whatever it is I challenge you to give it your all.

The second point I want to make, *Stay away from distractions.* Do not allow distractions to get you off your path. I remember us questioning my teammate. One thing that she mentioned was she looked to the side which was a distraction. When you are running your race you must stay focused straight ahead on reaching your goal or should I say reaching the finish line. Don't allow people or situations to distract you regardless of family, friends, or coworkers. You must stay away from distractions.

I can remember times in my life when I felt, 'this journey is getting a little heavy, but I can't give up ad quite I must keep pressing.' This brings me to my last point in this chapter, *Stay focused and do not quit.* There will be times during your journey that you may find yourself getting tired. I know I have experienced this feeling. I want to remind you that despite the obstacles that may come your way, you cannot get weary in well doing. You cannot quit when others quit, when things are not going as well as they are supposed to. You have to stay in the race no matter how many come and go, no matter how many walks away from you. It is up to you to stay on track, stay in your lane, and run at your pace.

I am going to end this chapter with one of my favorite poems by Edgar A. Guest.

"When things go wrong, as they sometimes will, When the road you're trudging seems all uphill, When the fund are low and debts are high, And you wan to Smile but have to sigh. When care is pressing you down a bit, Rest, if you must, but don't you quit.

"Life is queer with its twists and turns, As everyone of us sometimes learns, And many failure turns about, When he might have won if he'd stuck it out, Don't give up through the pace seems slow, You might succeed with another blow.

"Success is failure turned inside out, the silver tint of the clouds of doubt, and when you never can tell how close you are, it may be near when it seems afar; so stick to the fight when you're hardest hit, it's when things seem worst, you must not quit."

Remember, stay in your lane. Be encouraged, and know God is with you. The race is not given to the quick, nor the powerful, but to those who persevere until the end. Finish strong on whatever it is that you are trying to achieve in the season. Be encouraged in knowing that God loves you. I pray he continues to bless you. I handed the torch over to you, and I hope that you run with all that is in you.

Grab Your Pen & Work The Principle

I AM Staying In My Lane

May God bless you. May God keep you. That is my prayer, in Jesus name.

PRINCIPLE #6

I AM

I AM is an interactive guide teaching others how to work the principles for a better life. I want to dedicate this chapter to sharing who I AM and how I have applied the principles into my everyday life.

The most important things that I am is a wife, mother, and daughter. I want to discuss the portion of being a daughter with you all first. I was blessed to be raised in a two-parent household by my parents Calvin and Shirley Wilson. My parents are very influential to my success. They have always been very active in my life. They supported me through out my endeavors and they continued to do so even when I became an adult. My family life has always been good until 2022.

My father received an unexpected diagnosis of stage 4 pancreatic cancer. This news shocked our family and turned our world upside down. Prior to my father's diagnosis, he lived life to the fullest. We would take family vacations. He loved attending basketball games and visiting family. Sadly, all that changed when we received the terrible news that he had pancreatic cancer. Unfortunately, his last days came 40 days later on May 24th, 2022. Despite this tragedy, I am thankful for the blessing I received from God, and I will forever cherish it. I have always been a Daddy's Girl and there isn't a day that passes by that I don't think about my father.

After the passing of my father, I became an Author. In the midst of my grief God birthed a beautiful 40-day devotional titled Daddy's Girl.
The thought of writing a 40-day devotional for women came to me in 2020. I had it on my vision board. I was turning 40 that year, twenty plus twenty equals 40. I had all the signs, but I couldn't find the time to start writing. The devotional didn't come into fruition until two years later during the grieving process. As a result, you are now looking at a source of encouragement and inspiration for women all over who have experienced pain such as mine, whether it is from the loss of their father, longing for a

relationship with their father, or never knowing their father. Regardless, we are all Daddy's girls, because we are created in the image and likeness of our Heavenly Father GOD.

Let me explain how the devotional works: it contains prayers, affirmations, and scriptures for every day. I did this because I understand the impact of our words. When I went through grief over my own losses, it was the power of my words that kept me going. Each day I told myself, "April, you are a mother, and your daughters are depending on you. You are a wife, and your husband needs you. You're an entrepreneur and others are counting on you. The I AM within me stood up and I squared my shoulders back and held my head up high and started moving forward. I realized taking out the pen and paper was a healing tool for me. I still find it very encouraging to this day.

I AM an entrepreneur. Every morning before I start my day I take time to pray or meditate and commune with the Father. I try to focus on God's calling and HIS will for my life on that day. The journey of becoming an entrepreneur has been a long one for me. It involved tears, self-doubt, and many years of hard work. On my vision board I wrote for years that I would be an entrepreneur, and now it has been over 10 years since I started working for myself! It wasn't easy but the hard work and dedication allowed the words to come into alignment and eventually the words I spoke manifested in my life.

I never wavered in my faith instead I put my faith into action, and I worked the principles that you will learn in this book. I believed it and acted on that belief. I have always been big on vision boards. I can remember adding RED lipstick and RED colored kisses to my vision board. I added those items for two consecutive years. This was to demonstrate my desire to have my own lipstick brand one day. In 2022 A'Lashell was birth in the midst of me grieving the passing of my father and enduring life storms. During this time, God granted me beauty for ashes. My father had always been there, telling me that I could do it, vouching for my visions and ambitions. Even after his passing, I couldn't allow his support of me to die with him, so I did what he believed in me to do. I made it happen with the GRACE of GOD.

I made a pledge to attain those dreams and visions. What you see before you are my success, guaranteed to get even bigger and better than I could ever imagine or anticipate. Everything starts with having a thought in mind. Take the time to think about what you want to do, and believe that you can make it happen. Recognize the potential inside of yourself, and don't be afraid to go for it. Think about what it is that you want to achieve today and how to get there, even if there are roadblocks in your way.

I didn't expect it, but God orchestrated everything from the beginning to the end. I started writing down my vision and believed in it, speaking it into existence. It didn't all happen quickly; in fact, it took place at an unexpected time. I was still grieving the loss of my father when something new began to materialize. Who could've predicted that something so special would be born out of such a difficult season?

My journey may be an inspiration for you, so take this as encouragement and start working towards what God is calling you to do in this life time. This is just a glimpse of who I AM. There is so much more inside of me that one day I will share. I hope the words written thus far have blessed you and will inspire you to go after everything God said you can obtain. I pray you will be blessed and encouraged to work the principles.

Grab Your Pen & Work The Principle

I AM

PRINCIPLE #7

I AM Doing a New Thing

I have a word for you. Grab your Bible and turn to Isaiah 43:19. This is taken from the New English Translation, *For I am about to do something new. See, I have already begun!* Do you not see it? The Lord said, *For I am about to do something new,* then he said, *I have already begun.* We are catching up to what God has already done in our lives. We must catch up to the new things that He is trying to give us.

The word says, *do you not see it?* Question? Do you not see what God is doing in your life? You have not even imagined what he is calling for you to accomplish in this season. Let's skip down to verse 20 (b); *Yes, I will make rivers in the dry wasteland so my chosen people can be refreshed.* Hold up, wait a minute, He said, *so my chosen people can be refreshed.* God will supply everything that we need. He will make a way out of no way just for you. We are his chosen people.

At this point in my life, I finally understand that God wants to do a new thing in our lives. In 2022 God blessed me to be able to do 8 new things. Let me give you examples, so you can really understand God is doing new things in our lives. The good news is HE wants to do even more.

1. I wrote my first book titled Daddy's Girl.

2. I started my own lipstick brand, A'Lashell.

3. I made a Divine Connection with a Business Mentor.

4. I started Dr. April Webster Ministry and YouTube channel.

5. I held my first event Dr. April Webster Holiday Mixer.

6. I launched my new website for A'Lashell.

7. I launched my new website for Dr. April Webster Ministries.

8. I spoke international at a Women's Retreat in Mexico. I traveled several times by myself for business meeting and events.

I only provided 8 new things as an example, but I had at least five more that I could share. I shared all of that because every example that I gave you was God ordained. If it had not been for God, I wouldn't have had the strength to take the necessary steps to embrace those new things. Now I am open to new connection that are aligned by God. I want to encourage you to embrace the NEW.

The principle that I want to write down is learning to embrace new things. It is important for us to continue growing and developing. As we grow we must be willing to learn and accept new things as they come our way. I am excited that I applied this principle to my life in 2022. I didn't allow myself to be buried in grief but instead I learn to accept the new normal and reflect on the memories of my father.

I believe God wants us to realize the new things he is doing in our lives. You must be willing to try new things and invest in yourself in ways you have never done before. If I did not submit myself to the will of God, I would not be able to share my testimony with you today.

I want to challenge you to try something new. Write down at least six things. Write down at least six things that you are planning on doing this year. If it is making new connections, if it is setting a new goal, anything, write it down. Be willing to work on something new with God. Throughout this year just continue writing new things down as they occur and at the end of the year total all the new things you have accomplished. It doesn't matter if it is something big or small write it down.

Grab Your Pen & Work The Principle

I AM Doing A New Thing

May God bless you, and may God preserve you. I hope that you are blessed. I hope you are going to make something new. I am doing a new thing.

PRINCIPLE *#8*

I AM Letting It Go

Today, get your pen ready! It's time to let go of some things. Be sure to write down these words in the note section of this chapter. Please understand you cannot bring old baggage into a new season. It's time for us to prepare to de-clutter somethings in our lives to make room for new things. This chapter focus on the principle of letting go. Take a moment to think about things in your life that you need to let go. It can be relationships, clothes that you haven't worn in years, it can be bad habits. Whatever it is I want you to write those things in the note section and give it an eviction notice. It's time to let it go!

It's time to free yourself from people who are on a different path then you. Let go of the hurt, drama, and issues of your past. It is essential to not cling on to things that don't serve you, your time, or your attention. Don't be held back by old friends who aren't going in the same direction as you. Take this as an example: In Mark 5th chapter. When Jesus was on his way to Jairus' house due to Jarius daughter being sick to the point of death, those around him were saying 'don't bother Jesus, she is already dead'. But what did Jesus do? He looked at Jarius and said, "Do not be afraid, only believe." They continued walking to Jarius house, when they arrived they were greeted by mourners at the door.

They were weeping and saying the little girl was dead. But Jesus rebuked them and summoned only Peter, James, and John. He could have chosen any of the disciples, but he selected the ones that had Faith to believe.

I want to encourage every reader to give yourself permission to forgive others and release them from any past pain. This principle is sometime one of the hardest for people. But letting go is a principle that we must use in our lives in various seasons.

I strongly urge you to let go of issues of the past that can hinder your progress and growth. Letting go can be a freeing and revitalizing experience; it doesn't have to be yours to hold on to. Think about what is holding you back from achieving your goals and work toward releasing it. Let go of any lingering grudges or hurt feelings you may be holding on to and allow yourself time to heal and forgive. Remind yourself that yes, they hurt you, but it's best for you to release that pain and move forward.

It's important to recognize the people who have your best interests at heart. Allow this year to be the year you surround yourself with like-minded individuals. We must walk by faith and not sight and trust in God's plan for our lives. I am being intentional on letting go of any baggage others may have placed upon me on my journey. I am trusting in God by faith to make every crooked place straight.

On thing I have realized, we cannot allow ourselves to carry old baggage into a new season. Those bags from the past will weigh you down. So, get rid of that load. Picture it in your mind and serve it an eviction notice; no longer will it dwell here. As you release this weight, consider this:

It is okay to release any emotions you are feeling whether it be an outward expressing like *crying, writing, or praying.* All these forms of releasing can help bring positive outcomes and lead to the best possible result. I want to encourage you today to apply theses three things to ensure that you are letting go of the past and those feelings that have been weighing you down.

Don't be afraid of crying when something or someone has hurt you or when you are letting something or someone go. Crying has the ability of releasing oxytocin and endogenous opioids, otherwise known as endorphins. These feel-good chemicals can help a person ease their pain both physically and emotionally. When we cry, we take in quick breaths of cool air. Breathing in cooler air can help regulate and even lower the temperature of our brain. Crying is a form of releasing and often this is for our own good. And don't forget about praying for that thing and then trusting God with it.

The second principle in letting go is writing it out. Writing things out is very beneficial. Allowing our emotions to flow through writing is a form of release. The benefit to writing things down helps bring clarity to situations. When you take time to write things down such as your thoughts, feelings, emotions, etc., you're able to reflect on what has happened and even allow yourself to express your true feelings. When you put the pen to the paper you are able to have control over the situation. When letting go of past hurts I believe it's a good idea to write how you feel on paper and then put it in the trash. That is a form of releasing and letting whatever happen be put away. It no longer has the power to control you. If there is anything that you know you need to let go, take time and write it in the note section. Then later take a moment to express your true feelings. Once you have finished then tear it up, ball it up, or rip it up and place it in the trash. Allow yourself to release it so you can move forward.

The last principle in letting go is praying. There is no denying that relationships can come to an end, but it is important to be prayerful. When we must let people, careers, whatever go in our lives we must be prayerful. Praying is a very important principle in letting go. I urge you to embrace when we have to let things go by cry it out, writing it out, and praying it out. Whatever principle works best for you. Furthermore, don't forget to forgive yourself and take responsibility for your part. Take a moment to inhale and exhale deeply; letting go of anything preventing you from progressing and moving forward. Remember, God loves you and he wants us to experience the best that life has to offer us and that may require letting some things go in order to receive all that He has for us.

Grab Your Pen & Work The Principle

I AM Letting It Go

____

____

____

____

____

____

____

____

____

____

____

____

____

____

____

____

____

____

____

____

____

____

____

____

____

God bless you. May God keep you.

I AM A Survivor

Let's talk about being a survivor. I'm sure you can understand why I believe we are survivors. After all, we made it through Covid-19 that took the lives of millions of people worldwide. To survive something means to continue living through difficult times. Since you are reading this book that is exactly what we have done!

All of us have faced a hardship at some point in our lives. Whether during the pandemic, career change, the loss of a loved one, or any other setback. Destiny's Child was American musical girls' group that had a song titled *"Survivor."* I want to emphasize the chorus that says, "I'm not going to give up. I'm not going to stop. I'm going to work harder." Those are the 3 principles to apply when you are a Survivor.

I know this from personal experience, particularly when my father passed away. I found myself going through a dark moment in my life. I have never lost anyone that close to me in my life. I am grateful that God gave me strength daily and I didn't give up. But instead, I wrote my first book entitled, *Daddy's Girl.* I started my lipstick brand named A'Lashell. These things were birth during a dark season in my life. I didn't have time to give up. I know my father wouldn't have wanted that for my life, so I worked harder and shifted my thoughts to positive things. In times of difficulty God will exchange your beauty from the ashes. Can I encourage someone who may be dealing with a difficult situation, take time to breath, pray, and don't give up.

I refused to allow that situation to make me give up, and I want you to understand that no matter what you had to go through in the last year, you have made it through. You have survived! That means no matter your personal sickness or any illnesses experienced by you or a family member, such as cancer, chemo and radiation treatments - the fact that you are still here with breath in your body is proof of your resilience. So don't lose hope! What's next? Let's take action. Don't stay stuck anymore; move forward as a survivor. Realize that it is with movement that you gain momentum, progress and new opportunities.

It's okay to take a break, or even change direction. But it's not alright to stay where you are. Like they said in the song: "I'm not going to stop/We're not going to stop". When my father passed away, I could easily have gone down a dark path and let sadness consume me. But I kept pushing forward instead – and soon I'll explain why that's so important. If you're still alive, there must be something keeping you here - a reason for you to continue and keep striving. So don't give up, don't quit fighting; carry on no matter what! That's why the next point is clear: I'm going to move ahead and work even harder.

Excuse me - that's the one I wanted to get to. Everything I said in the beginning was to make sure this third point could be properly conveyed: you need to work harder in 2023 than you did in 2022. Whatever successes you achieved last year are commendable, but you need to keep putting your all into it, investing in yourself and pushing forward. Never allow yourself to feel as though you have 'arrived' because there is always more room for improvement and development - more people who can benefit from your efforts and more of your own inner potential that needs to be realized. As a living witness here before you, I am dedicating my own self to working even harder this year than ever before - striving for victory after victory and championship after championship!

Just like Michael Jordan did with the number 23, he worked hard and never gave up. He didn't stop and say, "I've done enough; I have enough rings". Instead, he kept pushing forward, continuing to put his all into every endeavor. That is what is expected of us as survivors; we don't quit even when times get tough, we work harder, give it everything we have. I implore you to apply these principles in all aspects of life, live it fully and never underestimate your own potential!

You have not yet seen the fullness of God and all that He has planned for you. As long as you are still here, there is still more to do. Will you get back in the game? Get yourself kitted up; put on your running shoes, your basketball shoes, or your football cleats. Do not give up; we have been given a chance to survive, so use it. Put in the work and give it all you have got!

As a survivor of the sudden loss of my father, I understand the power that grief can have. In those 40 days, it shook my world, and I could have allowed myself to give up, but I didn't. Instead, it birthed something incredible: me talking to you today, coming out of the dark place after all this time. Therefore, if you are ever in a low place or going through a difficult moment in your life, I urge you to rise above it and come out better on the other side. Today is the day to begin anew. Thank you for joining me here today; I'm so excited for what lies ahead!

The time is now for you to get up. The time is now because you survived it. You survived it. You've had another chance. You have a, you have breath in your body. It is a new day, a new day to start again, a new day, to press forward a new day, to keep it moving a new day that is filled with the full potential of so much more. I want to encourage you not to give up, not to stop, but in this season you have to work harder. We are survivors. Let's get to work and put our hands to everything that God is calling us to do in this year.

Grab Your Pen & Work The Principle

I AM A Survivor

May God bless you.

I AM Blessed

Grab your pen; I want to share with you a word God has given me. Write these words in the note section, *I AM Blessed.* Yes. I'm talking about you. Do you understand that you are blessed? We are called to walk in the fullness of God and all that he has for us. That includes blessings, upon blessings, upon blessings. It is our portion, and it is due to us. Blessings are gifts from God that bring happiness and joy into our lives. God blesses us with his favor, to fulfill his plan for our lives. He blesses those who trust and obey his word.

The Bible is full of verses regarding blessings. We should meditate on what the Bible says about who we are and the blessings that is upon us. Allow the word of God to convert your thinking. We are Blessed. It's time for us to start acting like we understand the blessings upon us.

One of my favorite stories in the Bible can be found in Genesis 37. This chapter is about a man named Joseph. He was a man that was favored by his father and God. He was his father Jacob favorite son. Jacob gave Joseph a gift which was a coat of many colors.

When you're blessed and favored, there will be people that will not like you. In the story Joseph's brothers hated him. They plotted to get rid of him by throwing him into a pit because of his divine favor. I'm here to tell you that it could very well be you who is chosen, the one meant to bless your family. You could be the Joseph of your generation and provide blessings to others.

In the story of Joseph, we also learn that his brothers threw him into a pit and sold him into slavery. Joseph had several things working against him with his brothers. He was favored by their father, he received a coat of many colors, and he shared his dream with his brothers. Despite this, when Joseph shared his dream with them, they were not supportive, and it only exacerbated their hatred towards him. We must be careful who we share our dreams and vision with because not everyone will supportive or happy for you.

You must acknowledge that no matter who you are, blessings do not come merely from yourself. The truth is all our blessings come from the Lord. I believe before the world even existed; blessing was poured out upon over lives before the foundation of this world. I know this may sound cliché but GOD has a blessing with your name on it just like He did Joseph.

Please note blessings doesn't just mean material riches; blessings come in many forms. God extends both spiritual and natural blessings. Your presence alone can bring light and joy to those around you, giving them an opportunity to learn more about the God you serve. When you enter the room, people recognize that there is something special about this man or woman. So yes, while financial blessings are a part of it, there's so much more that comes with being blessed by the Lord!

Understand this when God can trust you to be a blessing to others, that's when you access a whole new level of Divine blessing. This means you have the opportunity to give in abundance—love, counsel, wisdom and so much more. I can write, I AM BLESSED, and I know it to be true. I have experienced ups and downs, yet I remain blessed, nonetheless.

Have I experience some difficult times? Absolutely. Am I still abundantly blessed? Again, Absolutely. Gratitude should come hand-in-hand with being blessed. I understand if it wasn't for the Lord, I wouldn't be able to share my testimony with you all. It is part of being blessed accepting the blessings that come with saying 'Yes' to God's will. When I was a young girl, I already knew I was blessed. Now, that I have grown and developed into an adult I understand blessings. I understand my obedience to God's plan for my life has allowed blessing to continue to flow.

When you submit to God's will and accept His plan for your life, you will be blessed. In this season, it is important to understand who we are called to be and appreciate the fact that we are chosen to be blessed. I want to challenge you to wake up each morning embracing the fact that you are blessed. Let us walk throughout our day being thankful for everything God has bestowed upon us. Start your day expecting a blessing and acknowledging Him for every miraculous encounter.

In understanding that we are a blessed people, we are a chosen generation, and called to be a blessing to others. We are called for greater. If I may submit to you today, in case you did not realize who you were, I want you to know that you are blessed. The time has come for you to walk into God's blessings.

I want to end this *chapter with Deuteronomy 28:1-8 New King James Version of the Bible. "Now it shall come to pass, if you diligently obey the voice of the Lord your God, to observe carefully all His commandments which I command you today, that the Lord your God will set you high above all nations of the earth. And all these blessings shall come upon you and overtake you, because you obey the voice of the Lord your God.*

"Blessed shall you be in the city, and blessed shall you be in the country. Blessed shall be the fruit of your body, the produce of your ground and the increase of your herds, the increase of your cattle and the offspring of your flocks. Blessed shall be your basket and your kneading bowl. Blessed shall you be when you come in, and blessed shall you be when you go out.

"The Lord will cause your enemies who rise against you to be defeated before your face; they shall come out against you one way and flee before you seven ways. The Lord will command the blessing on you in your storehouses and in all to which you set your hand, and He will bless you in the land which the LORD your God is giving you."

Write in big bold letters, I AM BLESSED!

Grab Your Pen & Work The Principle

I AM Blessed

May God bless you. It is my prayer in Jesus' name. God bless you.

PRINCIPLE #11

I AM Connected

Featuring LaShawn Webster

The connection I have with my husband LaShawn Webster is a divine connection. Have you ever heard the term "a match made in Heaven?" There are some connections that are so powerful and intense that they appear to be divine. We are going to share our story in these last two chapters. A divine connection generally refers to a spiritual or religious connection or bond.

God has divine connections lined up for our lives. God has made it clear that there are things we can't control and don't have any other choices than to believe, obey, and pray. There is power in connections. Here is our story!

Lashawn Webster: I knew right away that I wanted to marry April. From the very first time that we met, maybe within 48 hours of knowing her, I had a sense of peace. She just has this connection with God that is simply unmatched. We could be in a room together and nothing had to be said for hours and it felt like home, like we were destined to be together for the rest of our lives.

April Webster: God had something special in store for Shawn and I. When we first started dating in 2015, it was an immediate connection. Our chemistry was so strong. It was a sacred link between us that contributed to our individual development on all levels. In Ecclesiastes 4:9-12 NKJV, reminds us, *"Two are better than one, because they have a good reward for their labor. For if they fall, one will lift up his companion. But woe to him who is alone when he falls. For he has no one to help him up. Again, if tow lie down together, they will keep warm, but how can one be warm alone? Through one may be overpowered by another, two can withstand him and a threefold cord is not quickly broken."* We realized early on that our connection was bigger than us. We had to separate for some years, but God allowed our divine connection to come full circle. I realized that detachment was beneficial to our growth and development as individuals. We stayed connected throughout the years via my cousin Ahmad. We would check on each other. We never completely closed the door. We reconnected in 2019 and it was like we had never separated. We were married in 2020 and the rest is history. Shawn will share our story on how we birth A'Lashell lipstick brand, through our divine connection with God in 2021.

Lashawn Webster: I loved my wife's red lipstick; I thought it would be only right for her to have her own lipstick brand. She has beautiful lips. Her favorite color is Red. She is a member of Delta Sigma Theta. I thought she should have her own brand. So, with that in mind, I decided to call it A'Lashell. April is her first name, and LaShell is her middle name. It flowed very well, and we started putting it on our vision boards, as well as on our prayer list. In 2021 it was birthed and now we can see and hold the words we have spoken and written. I'm proud of our product but most importantly I'm proud of my wife.

April Webster: As my husband mentioned we had A'Lashell and red lipstick on our vision board for over two years. I want to share a principle with you all at this point. The first thing I did after my husband sown the seed that I should start my own lipstick brand I believed it. I would like you to write in the note section the word Believe. You must first believe in yourself. Once my husband said it, I believe that I could do it. I started putting my faith into action. I wrote A'Lashell on my vision board. I started praying over A'Lashell. Because of my connection to my husband and him planting the seed A'Lashell was birthed. I want you to think about the people you feel divinely connected too and why. Write down in the note section why you are connected to each of them; this list can include your spouse, mother, sibling, or anyone that comes to mind. If your reason doesn't include God, then reassess that list. We can see an example of a God-given connection between Shawn and I. He knew within 48 hours I was going to be his wife in spite of the separation that came in between our relationship for four years. He still Believed.

I knew we had a special connection during our years apart. I kept asking myself, "What if this is my husband? What should I do differently? What could I have changed?" As I prayed and sought God's guidance, the same energy and connection returned when we met again four years later. Consider the people you are connected to and why. If it is for something greater than yourself, have faith and believe that God will make it come full circle.

Lashawn Webster: Your influence is affected by those you associate with. Take the time to contemplate who your circle of connections is. I recently discussed this with our daughter Nyjha, and she suggested a few names. Once you really think it through, it's possible to make the changes needed and cut ties or in the words of my wife "LET GO" of anyone who's in your life. Negative impacts are not worth it, while maintaining relationships with those who bring out the best in you.

April Webster: It's important to consider who you're connected to in life. This may involve changes in connections as we take on our appointed paths. To that end, my husband suggested asking our daughter (who at this time is 15) at one point: "Who's in your circle? Are they helping you reach your potential?" If not, the answer could be to check the circle and, if necessary, make changes.

Lashawn Webster: Yes, it is essential to push yourself out of your comfort zone. My wife helps me a great deal in this regard; she sees potential in me that I may not have noticed myself. Not that I don't think I'm capable, but when you couple that capability with the connection and love of someone else who is also growth oriented, then you are able to reach heights you may never have thought possible. Moreover, if they are on a different path than yours, it is best to simply accept them as they are and move on. In other words, you cannot attempt to control or manipulate individuals; instead, if you appreciate them for who they truly are, chances are the right people will come into your life eventually.

April Webster: It's very important to allow people to be who they are. If my husband had not allowed me to stay true to the authentic April, our relationship wouldn't have survived. That April is bold, loves the Lord and isn't afraid of claiming her space in a room and getting involved without being invited. When in a connection with someone, like my spouse, it's necessary to stay aligned and in agreement. The Bible confirms it: how can two walk together unless they be in agreement? Fortunately, God has blessed me with a strong man who understands that He has called us for a greater purpose. My husband walks beside me into unknown opportunities and doors, supporting my ambitions, and trusting that the world will witness our greatness. My husband walks in that alignment. He understands that there is greater on the inside of us, individually and collectively that has to come out for this world to see. He is connected to me spiritually and naturally.

Lashawn Webster: It's all about us being here, and how we supplement each other in various aspects. For instance, her love for preaching and my passion in studying. We didn't know each other had those interests until much later but God knew. I think it's essential to keep an open mind and maybe someone is just meant to be your friend or even a distant acquaintance, not necessarily a partner in marriage. But she knew that we were going to get married eventually! That's another topic.

April Webster: Today, I want to remind you of the importance of understanding your divine connections and why. Investigate your circle, see if the people you are currently connected to can help you reach the next level in your life. Your connections can either be a blessing or a hindrance: it's been a blessing for us! We encourage other couples to get to know each other and fully understand God's calling for them together.

Lashawn Webster: I'd like to encourage you to allow God to guide you through the person you should be with. Because if you truly listen and open your mind, your heart, and your spirit to God, guidance will come. Follow directions, you must follow HIS directions. I remember hearing very clearly from GOD that I had to go to April. I remember hearing it like it was yesterday and I obeyed the voice of the Lord.

April Webster: Therefore, as he stated, he listened to the voice of God. Being connected to a person means being in tune to what God says about them. He would not have come back to me if God hadn't told him too. I am grateful that my husband inclined his ears to hear what the Lord was saying to him pertaining to his wife. Remember connections matter!

Grab Your Pen & Work The Principle

I AM Connected

I AM Enough

Featuring LaShawn Webster

My husband LaShawn, is joining me in this chapter, sharing the principle of I AM Enough. It's important for us to truly comprehend that we are enough. We are people created in the image and likeness of God. Before entering any relationship, one must realize who they are and understand the principle that they are enough.

To illustrate this idea, think of the scripture passage where Jesus is with his disciples, who are being asked by him: "Who do men say that I am?" Answers like John the Baptist, a prophet or Elijah were mentioned, yet Jesus knew only one person was able to correctly identify Him. And that person was Peter, who answered "You are the son of God." My purpose here is to encourage you to know yourself so that when others encounter you, they will know you are more than enough.

Understand that you are worthy, deserving to be who God has called you to be. Today, I know I am enough as a wife, mother, entrepreneur, Evangelist, Author, and so much more. As I mentioned in the previous chapter my husband and I had a diving connection. From the moment we met I knew he was more than enough for me. He possessed the ability, expertise, and intelligence that I needed in a spouse. God certainly exceeded my expectations with my husband.

LaShawn Webster: I think to really be enough, you must first understand your own worth as a child of God. Everything that you need is already inside of you, so it's all about channeling it in the right way and having faith in yourself. To make this faith solid, you must recognize the truth about God and recognize that there is room for everyone to achieve greatness. You must stay confident, not wavering; decide if the direction you are going is correct and stay focused. A double-minded man is unstable in all ways.

Having someone to guide you is certainly helpful. But it is important to be aware of the internal doubts that can arise and try to shake them off. I always advise April, channel your thoughts and energy into something productive. Be sure to stay on the straight path with faith in the creator, being secure in yourself rather than letting external factors make you second guess something. Anything outside of ourselves can make us doubt ourselves, but if we focus on what's within, then we will remain strong. That has been my experience.

April Webster: Let us have a brief discussion about self-worth, and how you can be sure of your value in whatever God has called upon you to do. It is within us all to possess the creative ability to achieve our aims in life. You are enough. Within you is everything required, as well as being worthy, blessed, and chosen by God. It can be helpful to recognize certain principles that remind us we have what it takes to accomplish every assigned God has planned for us.

LaShawn Webster: A key principle to remember is that bad times can often lead to good. It's something ingrained in God's laws and principles, and it's important to not get bogged down in our negative emotions during those difficult moments. Instead, we need to understand that these downs are a necessary part of life and will bring us closer to the good things. We must stay emotionally aware but not get stuck in our feelings, so that our understanding of this principle helps guide us through dark times and towards brighter days. When you find yourself in a bad place, shift your energy and practice thankfulness. Being grateful for the little things like your wife, children, home and lifestyle can make a huge difference. That alone is enough. Even if you don't reach all of your goals each day, sticking to these principles will create peace of mind for yourself and for your family. This will make everything on this earth seem easier. So just remember to be thankful every day.

April Webster: Remember, your worth is not diminished by any setback or hardship you may face. Your circumstances don't disqualify you from all that God has planned for you, so today focus on that know your worth.

When I met my husband, I was praying for someone who would meet my standards and deserve all of me. Knowing one's worth means not settling for less than you deserve. Do not lower your expectations; the one who is meant to be with you will meet your expectations. You are worthy of being celebrated, cherished, and loved, and whoever comes into your life should know this. When I think about my husband, I'm so thankful to have him. He was more than enough in every area and I'm grateful he listened to the voice of the Lord.

You are enough means that you don't have to strive to become worthy, accepted, loved, or valid. You are already all of those things and you must believe it for yourself. It is not a mistake that you are reading this chapter. You are enough as you are. You are enough means you can grow and change and continue to become and evolve. As messed up as some of us may have been, beautiful and broken, we are still enough.

You were enough before, you are enough now, and you will continue to be enough as you grow and emerge into becoming who God ordained you to be. You must remember to be content and satisfied with who you are. It's all about have a positive mindset and believing in yourself.

Grab Your Pen & Work The Principle

I AM Enough

ABOUT THE AUTHOR

Dr. April Webster is a native of Hickman, Ky. She is a devoted wife, mother, and mentor. She is an author, community leader, entrepreneur, and an ordained evangelist. April has a passion for serving others and helping them reach their highest potential in every aspect of their lives.

April is devoted to higher education and achievement. She obtained her Ph.D in Christian Psychology on May 11, 2011 from International College of Ministry. She holds a Master's Degree in Public Administration specializing in Human Resources, and a Bachelor of Arts Degree in Social Work both from Kentucky State University in Frankfort, Ky.

As an Author, Dr. Webster has published her first book titled Daddy's Girl.

Daddy's Girl is a collection of 40 days' worth of journal entries meant to inspire and instill hope in readers all around. Through personal anecdotes followed by supplications and affirmations.

As an Entrepreneur, she is the co-owner of Loving Arms, LLC home care agency founded in 2012. The agency provides quality services to adults with intellectual and developmental disabilities as well as the elderly population.

In 2022, Dr. Webster founded A'Lashell Cosmetics. She ventured into the world of beauty after a 20 plus year career in health care and social services. The idea was planted by her husband LaShawn Webster. April believed and birthed A'Lashell. The mission of A'Lashell is to enhance the natural beauty of women everywhere by encouraging and empowering them too boldly be confident within themselves. I AM Beautiful, Blessed, and Bold are the hallmarks of A'Lashell.

As an Evangelist, she is a positive influencer known for her passion and enthusiastic deliverance of the word of God. She has an uncanny ability to reach people from various walks of life.

In 2022, she birthed Dr. April Webster LLC. It is a ministry designed to empower, encourage, and equip people all over to reach their God-given potential by working the principles of faith. The ministry is a registered organization with the state of Tennessee.

MY NOTES

MY NOTES